First Facts™

**Positively Pets**

# Caring for Your

# Dog

by June Preszler

**Consultant:**
Jennifer Zablotny, DVM
Member, American Veterinary Medical Association

Capstone
press®

Mankato, Minnesota

First Facts is published by Capstone Press,
151 Good Counsel Drive, P.O. Box 669, Mankato, Minnesota 56002.
www.capstonepress.com

*Library of Congress Cataloging-in-Publication Data*
Preszler, June, 1954–
    Caring for your dog / June Preszler.
    p. cm. —(First facts. Positively pets)
    Summary: "Describes caring for a dog, including supplies needed, feeding, cleaning,
health, safety, and aging"—Provided by publisher.
    Includes bibliographical references and index.
    ISBN-13: 978-0-7368-6385-8 (hardcover)
    ISBN-10: 0-7368-6385-0 (hardcover)
    1. Dogs—Juvenile literature.  I. Title. II. Series.
SF426.5.P73 2007
636.7—dc22                                                     2005035853

**Editorial Credits**
Becky Viaene, editor; Bobbi J. Wyss, designer; Kim Brown, illustrator; Kelly Garvin,
    photo researcher/photo editor

**Photo Credits**    155-7291
Capstone Press/Karon Dubke, 5, 6
Gem Photo Studio/Dan Delaney, 15
Getty Images Inc./Taxi/Denis Felix, 12–13
Norvia Behling, 7, 10–11, 14, 17, 18–19; Daniel Johnson, 9
Photodisc, 21
Shutterstock/Jiang JingJie, cover; Nici Kuehl, 20

Capstone Press thanks the Kind Veterinary Clinic, Saint Peter, Minnesota, for their assistance
with this book.

# Table of Contents

# So You Want to Own a Dog?

Dog owners walk their pets in your neighborhood. Dogs **fetch**, roll over, and lick their owners' faces.

You've always wanted a dog. Many dogs at **shelters** need homes. Or maybe your neighbor has puppies for sale. But are you ready for the **responsibility**?

Be patient with me. It may take me weeks to learn a new trick, such as fetching.

# Supplies to Buy

Dogs need certain supplies. Get dog food, bowls for food and water, and a dog bed for your pet. Don't forget a brush, a collar, an ID tag, and a leash.

Dog toys keep your pet busy. Chew toys help clean your dog's teeth. Your dog likes it when you play too. Throw a ball and wait for her to bring it back to you.

# Your Dog at Home

When your dog first comes home, he may feel lost or scared. Let your dog get used to his new home slowly. For a few days, keep your dog in a small room. Give your new friend plenty of attention.

He'll soon be ready to explore. Make sure things he shouldn't eat or chew on are put away.

I love praise and attention. If you tell me I've been good, I'll wag my tail. But if you scold me, I'll tuck my tail between my legs.

# Your Dog with Other Pets

There might be growls and nips when your dog meets other pets. Introduce your pets slowly. Don't leave them alone until they are used to each other. Even a friendly dog can be rough and hurt smaller animals.

Whenever there are two dogs, one of us will be the leader.

# Feeding Your Dog

Your dog needs food and fresh water each day. Most adult dogs eat twice a day, but growing puppies eat three times. Dog food bags tell you how much food to give your dog.

I love treats. But don't give me more than two a day or I could get sick or fat.

# Cleaning

Dogs love to roll and rub on the ground. They need help staying clean. Give your dog a bath with dog shampoo.

Cleaning up after your dog is a smelly but necessary job. Scoop up dog waste, especially during walks, so no one steps in it.

# A Visit to the Vet

Help your dog stay healthy by taking her to a **veterinarian**. Dogs should visit a vet at least once a year to get a checkup and shots.

At about six months old, dogs can be **spayed** or **neutered** to keep them from having puppies. These surgeries keep shelters from becoming crowded with unwanted puppies.

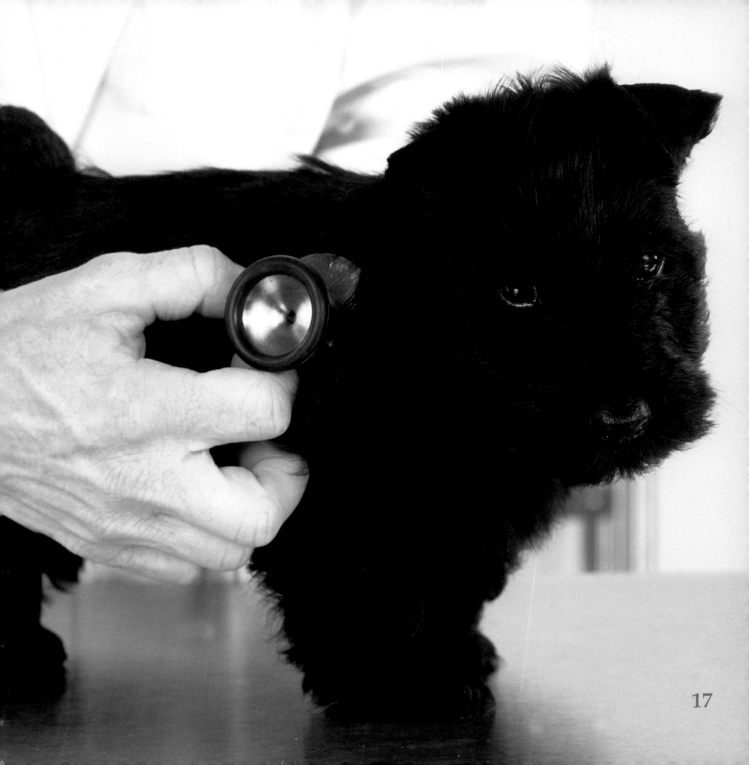

# Your Dog's Life

You and your dog will likely spend about 10 to 15 years together. As your dog gets older, she will sleep more and eat less.

Help your dog live a long and healthy life. Give her food, exercise, and regular checkups.

One of my years is like seven people years. When I am 10 years old, that's like 70 human years.

# Wild Relatives!

Most scientists believe that today's tame dogs came from grey wolves. Even today, grey wolves and dogs are a lot alike. They feed, play, howl, growl, and protect their **territory** in similar ways.

# Decode Your Dog's Behavior

- Dogs wag their tails fast to show they're excited. But a slow wag shows they are scared or upset.

- Be careful—angry or scared dogs are more likely to bite. Scared dogs lower their ears and tails. Angry dogs raise their tails, ears and fur, and may show their teeth.

- When dogs want to play, they drop their chests to the ground and raise their back ends in the air.

- Dogs bark for many reasons. A quick bark usually means a dog is playful. A long, high-pitched bark can mean a dog is upset.

# Glossary

**fetch** (FECH)—to go after and bring back something or somebody

**neuter** (NOO-tur)—to operate on a male animal so it is unable to produce young

**responsibility** (ris-spon-suh-BIL-uh-tee)—a duty or a job

**shelter** (SHEL-tur)—a place where homeless animals can stay

**spay** (SPAY)—to operate on a female animal so it is unable to produce young

**territory** (TER-uh-tor-ee)—an area of land that an animal claims as its own to live in

**veterinarian** (vet-ur-uh-NER-ee-uhn)—a doctor who treats sick or injured animals; veterinarians also help animals stay healthy.

# Read More

**Ganeri, Anita.** *Dogs.* A Pet's Life. Chicago: Heinemann, 2003.

**Hibbert, Clare.** *Dog.* Looking after Your Pet. North Mankato, Minn.: Smart Apple Media, 2005.

**Jeffrey, Laura S.** *Dogs: How to Choose and Care for a Dog.* American Humane Pet Care Library. Berkeley Heights, N.J.: Enslow, 2004.

# Internet Sites

FactHound offers a safe, fun way to find Internet sites related to this book. All of the sites on FactHound have been researched by our staff.

Here's how:

1. Visit *www.facthound.com*

2. Choose your grade level.

3. Type in this book ID **0736863850** for age-appropriate sites. You may also browse subjects by clicking on letters, or by clicking on pictures and words.

4. Click on the **Fetch It** button.

**FactHound will fetch the best sites for you!**

# Index